Meatball Mania!

Discover the Most Delicious and Easy

Meatball Recipes!

BY: Allie Allen

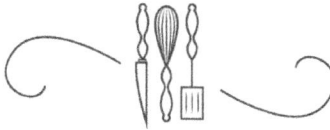

COOK & ENJOY

Copyright Notes

Table of Contents

Introduction

If you're looking for different ways to change up your usual dinner or lunch with a delicious meatball dish, look no further than this recipe book! This book consists of 30 delicious meatball recipes that will satisfy your taste buds and make them sing!

With this book, you'll be able to put up all sorts of delicious meatball recipes! All the recipes are detailed, easy-to-follow and versatile in nature and can be made by even the most beginner cook. So, choose a recipe and let's get started!

Sweet and Sour Meatballs

Sweet and sour Dutch oven meatballs with ginger, pineapple and chili sauce.

Makes: 6 servings

Prep: 10 mins

Cook: 1 hr.

Ingredients:

- 1 bag frozen meat balls, thawed
- ¼ cup chopped onion
- 1 8 oz. can pineapple tidbits
- 1 8 oz. jar grape jelly
- 1 bottle chili sauce
- 1 tsp. ground ginger

Directions:

Combine all ingredients in 10" Dutch oven with feet. Cover with flat lid. Arrange six coals in a circle and put Dutch oven on top of coals. Place ten additional hot coals around perimeter of the lid.

Bake for 1 hr., occasionally stirring gently. Replace with fresh hot coals as needed.

Serve hot over rice.

Meatball and Vegetable Soup

Easy 6-ingredient, one-pot soup recipe.

Makes: 6 servings

Prep: 5 mins

Cook: 20 mins

Ingredients:

- 3 (14-ounce) cans beef broth
- 1 (16-ounce) package frozen cooked meatballs, thawed
- 1 (15-ounce) can cannellini beans, rinsed & drained
- 1 can tomatoes with Italian herbs, undrained
- 1 (10-ounce) package frozen mixed vegetables, thawed
- 1 cup dried small pasta
- Freshly grated Parmigiano-Reggiano cheese to taste (optional)

Directions:

Add the broth, beans, meatballs, undrained tomatoes, and vegetables to a 4-quart Dutch oven over medium-high heat. Bring to boil & stir in the pasta. Return to boiling; reduce heat & simmer uncovered about 10 minutes or until the pasta is cooked.

To serve, ladle the soup into bowls. If desired, serve sprinkled with Parmigiano-Reggiano.

Garlic Tomato Sauce and Meatballs

Delicious recipe with garlic, tomato sauce and herbs.

Makes: 4 servings

Prep: 10 mins

Cook: 50 mins

Ingredients:

Sauce:

- 3 to 4 tbsp. extra-virgin olive oil
- 1/2 cup onion, chopped
- 4 cloves garlic, minced
- 1 tbsp. fresh Italian parsley, chopped
- 1 (8 oz.) can tomato sauce + scant can of water
- 1 (6 oz.) can tomato paste + scant can of water
- 1 tbsp. dried oregano
- 1/4 tsp. dried sweet basil
- 1 bay leaf
- 1/2 tsp. dried Italian seasoning
- 1/2 tsp. granulated sugar
- Salt and pepper, to taste

Meatballs:

- 1/2 lb. lean ground beef
- 2 cloves garlic, minced
- 1 egg, beaten
- 2 to 3 tbsp. water
- 1 cup plain dry breadcrumbs (add more as needed)
- 2 tbsp. Parmesan cheese, grated
- 1/4 tsp. dried oregano
- 1/2 tsp. fresh parsley, chopped
- 1/2 tsp. salt
- 1/4 tsp. pepper

Directions:

Sauce: Heat olive oil in a medium saucepan on high. Add onions and sauté 1 minute. Turn down heat to medium-high. Cook for 10 minutes or until beginning to brown. Add garlic, sauté about 5 minutes, or until both are golden brown (careful not to burn). Add fresh parsley and sauté just a few seconds. Add tomato sauce and paste. Fill cans with equal parts of water (scant) and add to sauce. Stir well until all lumps are dissolved. Add dried herbs by crushing between your hands. Add sugar, salt and pepper. Reduce heat to low & simmer 45 mins to 1 hour. Add cooked meatballs.

Meatballs: Add ground beef with remaining ingredients and mix well. Shape into 1 1/2 to 2-inch balls. Heat skillet with about 1 to 2 tbsp. olive oil. Place meatballs in pan and cook over medium-high heat, turning when meat loosens from pan. When done, remove & drain on paper towels. Add to sauce, stirring carefully.

To serve with cooked pasta: Place drained pasta in a pot. Toss with 1/2 cup sauce, coating the pasta with a light coating of sauce. Serve on plates and drizzle with a little more sauce on top. Sprinkle and garnish with fresh chopped basil and grated Parmesan/Romano cheese. Place any leftover sauce in a sauceboat or server.

Mostaccioli and Meatballs

Delicious meatball recipe with sausage, garlic and tomatoes.

Makes: 8 servings

Prep: 10 mins

Cook: 2 hrs. 40 mins

Ingredients:

Sauce:

- 1 to 2 lbs. mild sausage (may substitute 1/2 hot and 1/2 sweet sausage)
- 1 tbsp. parsley
- 2 tbsp. oregano
- 1/8 tsp. basil
- 6 large cloves garlic, minced
- 1 tsp. salt
- 3 (29 oz.) cans tomato puree
- 3 (6 oz.) cans tomato paste
- 1 onion, whole

Meatballs:

- 2 1/2 to 3 lbs. ground beef
- 3 eggs, beaten
- 1 (1.5 oz.) package meat loaf seasoning mix
- 2 cloves garlic, finely chopped
- 1 tbsp. parsley
- Salt and pepper, to taste
- 4 slices bread
- 1/2 cup milk
- 3/4 cup breadcrumbs
- 1/4 cup Parmesan cheese, grated

Pasta:

- 1 to 2 lbs. mostaccioli

Directions:

Cook the pasta; drain and set aside.

Sauce: Brown sausage in large pot. Cook, covered, for 30 minutes. Remove sausage, leaving most of the fat for flavor. Add parsley, oregano, basil, garlic and salt; stir. Add tomato puree and tomato paste; mix well. Fill both tomato puree and paste cans with water and add to sauce; mix well. Add whole onion (remove just before serving). Simmer at least 2 hours.

Meatballs: In a bowl, mix ground beef, eggs, seasoning mix, garlic, parsley, salt and pepper. In a bowl, soak slices of bread in milk. Squeeze out excess milk and break bread apart into small pieces. Combine bread, bread crumbs and Parmesan cheese. Add to ground beef and mix thoroughly. Shape into balls & bake at 350 degrees F. for 40 minutes. Add to sauce and serve over pasta.

Pasta: Prepare pasta according to package directions. Drain and rinse well with hot water. Return pasta to pan and stir in a small amount of sauce to prevent sticking. When serving, top with sauce.

Slow-Cooked Hearty Meatballs

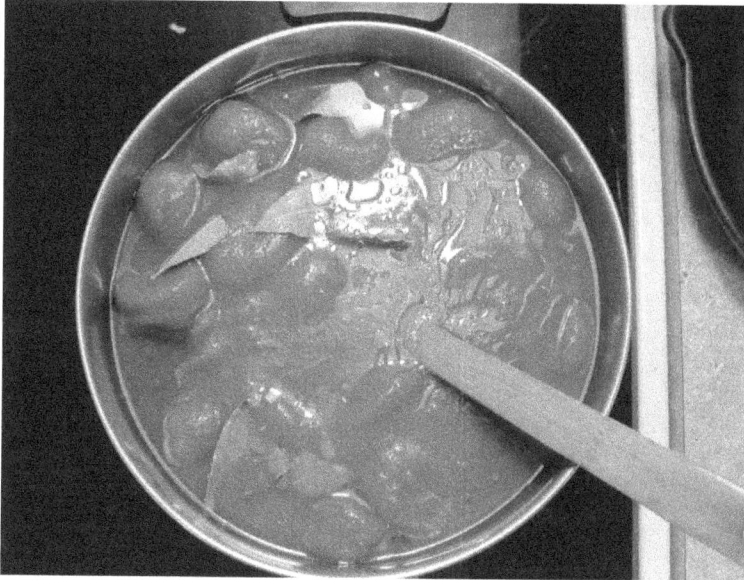

Slow cooked meatballs with rice, herbs and tomato juice.

Makes: 8 servings

Prep: 10 mins

Cook: 8 hrs.

Ingredients:

- 1 1/2 pounds lean ground beef
- 1 cup uncooked long-grain white rice
- 1 small yellow onion, peeled and finely chopped
- 3 cloves garlic, minced
- 2 tbsp. dried parsley
- 1/2 tbsp. dried dill
- 1 large egg
- 1/4 cup all-purpose flour
- 2 cups tomato juice or tomato-vegetable juice
- 2–4 cups water
- 2 tbsp. butter
- Salt to taste
- Freshly ground black pepper to taste

Directions:

Make meatballs by mixing together the ground beef with the rice, onion, garlic, parsley, dill, and egg in a large bowl; shape into small meatballs and roll each one in flour.

Add the tomato/tomato-vegetable juice to a 4-quart slow cooker. Add in the meatballs. Pour water to completely cover the meatballs. Add in the butter.

Cover & cook on low 6–8 hours, checking periodically to make sure the cooker doesn't boil dry. Add salt and pepper to taste.

Greek Meatball, Egg, and Lemon Soup

Greek-inspired meatball soup.

Makes: 6 servings

Prep: 10 mins

Cook: 7 hrs.

Ingredients:

- 1 pound lean ground beef
- 1 small yellow onion, peeled and minced
- 1 clove garlic, minced
- 6 tbsp. uncooked long-grain white rice
- 1 tbsp. dried parsley
- 2 tbsp. dried dill or mint
- 1 tsp. dried oregano
- Salt to taste
- 1/3 cup fresh lemon juice
- Freshly ground black pepper to taste
- 1 stalk celery, finely chopped
- 1 cup baby carrots, sliced
- 3 large eggs
- 4–6 cups chicken or vegetable broth
- 1 medium yellow onion, peeled and chopped
- 2 russet potatoes, peeled & cut into cubes
- 2 tbsp. corn flour

Directions:

In a bowl, combine together the meat, garlic, rice, minced onion, parsley, dill or mint, salt, oregano, pepper, and 1 egg. Shape into small meatballs and set aside.

Add 2 cups of broth/water to a slow cooker. Add in the meatballs, carrots, potatoes, chopped onion, and celery, then pour in enough of the remaining broth/water to cover the meatballs & vegetables. Cook on low 6 hours.

In a bowl, beat the two remaining eggs & then whisk in the corn flour. Slowly whisk in the lemon juice, & then ladle in about one cup of the hot broth from slow cooker, beating constantly until all has been put into the egg mix. Add this mixture into slow cooker. Continue to cook on low 1 hour or until thickened

Indonesian Meatballs with Pineapple Sauce

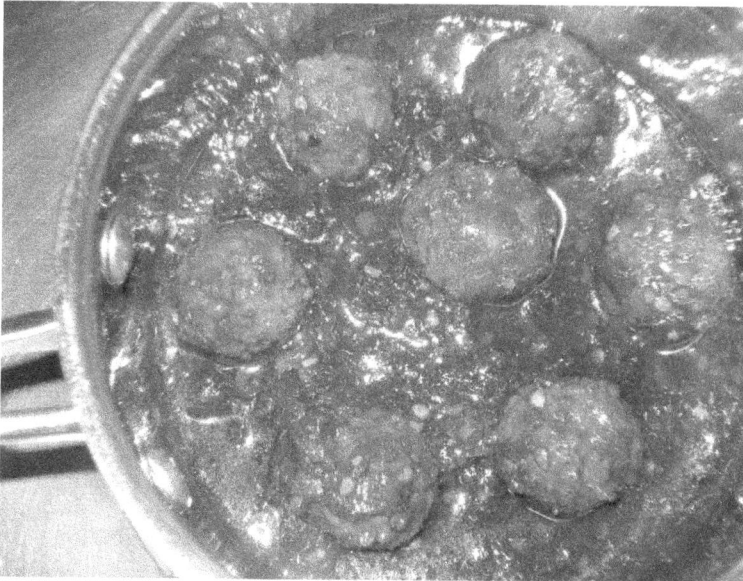

An appetizer meatball with a subtle blend of Far East flavors. Serve it in Pineapple Sauce, as shown below.

Makes: 6 servings

Prep: 10 mins

Cook: 1 hr.

Ingredients:

- 1 pound lean ground beef
- 1 cup GF breadcrumbs or GF cereal, crushed
- 1½ tbsp. curry powder
- 1 tbsp. peanut butter
- Salt and pepper to taste
- ½ tsp. ginger
- 2 tbsp. GF soy sauce
- ¼ tsp. garlic salt
- 1 egg
- 1 tbsp. dry milk powder
- 1 tsp. prepared mustard
- 1 tbsp. sesame or peanut oil, for frying

Pineapple Sauce

- 1 cup pineapple juice
- 2 tbsp. cornstarch
- 2 tbsp. lime juice
- 1 cup brown sugar
- 1 tsp. grated fresh gingerroot
- ¼ cup 7UP

Directions:

Put the pineapple juice in a small saucepan. In a bowl, blend together the cornstarch, lime juice, brown sugar, and ginger. Add to the pineapple juice. Cook until clear and slightly thickened. Remove from heat and add 7UP. Pour over the meatballs before baking.

Preheat oven to 350°.

Mix all of the ingredients apart from oil. Form into ¾-inch balls. Heat the oil in a heavy skillet and brown the balls, about a dozen at a time, shaking the skillet to keep them round. Cook only until the balls are browned and crusty. Remove the meatballs to a baking dish and fry the next batch.

When all the balls are done, bake for about 45 minutes, covered with the Pineapple Sauce, if desired. Or bake plain and serve with dipping sauces on the side.

Meatballs Mole

Don't pass up this excitingly different flavor in meatballs. The chocolate in the sauce spells Mexico. The Pre-Columbian Indians used chocolate as a spice long before the Europeans started adding sugar and making chocolate desserts. Serve with rice or spaghetti.

Makes: 4-6 servings

Prep: 10 mins

Cook: 1 hr. 15 mins

Ingredients:

Meatballs:

- 1 pound lean ground beef
- 1 egg, beaten
- ½ cup milk or nondairy liquid
- ¾ cup crushed corn chips
- 1 tsp. salt
- 2½ tbsp. rice flour
- 2 tbsp. vegetable oil

Sauce:

- 3 medium onions, chopped
- 1 clove garlic, minced
- 2 tbsp. sugar
- 1 tbsp. chili powder
- 1 tsp. ground cumin
- 1 tsp. ground coriander
- 1 tsp. dried oregano
- 1½ tbsp. salt
- One 16-ounce can tomato puree
- 1 square unsweetened chocolate
- 1 cup water

Directions:

Meatballs: In a bowl, mix the beef, egg, milk, corn chips, and salt. Mix until well combined. Refrigerate 1 hour.

Preheat oven to 350°.

Shape the mixture into 20 balls. Place flour in low, flat pan and roll the balls in it until coated (reserve remaining flour).

In a skillet/heavy Dutch oven, heat the oil and brown the meatballs, a few at a time. Remove as they brown to a 2½-quart casserole.

Sauce: In the same pan, sauté the onion and garlic until translucent. Remove pan from heat.

Combine the sugar, chili powder, cumin, coriander, oregano, salt, and the flour that remained from rolling the meatballs. Stir into the skillet along with the tomato puree, chocolate, and the water.

Return to heat and bring mixture to boiling, stirring constantly. Lower heat to a simmer, cover, & cook for 30 minutes, stirring occasionally. Put the sauce over the meatballs in the casserole and bake, covered, for 45 minutes.

NOTE: If you prefer, you may add the meatballs to the sauce in the skillet or Dutch oven and simmer, covered, for 30 minutes.

Mediterranean Turkey Meatballs

Meatballs with Mediterranean-inspired flavors.

Makes: 4 servings

Prep: 10 mins

Cook: 45 mins

Ingredients:

- 1¼ pounds ground turkey
- ½ cup grated onion
- 1 egg, beaten
- 1½ tbsp. chopped raisins
- 1 tbsp. chopped walnuts or pecans
- 1 tbsp. minced fresh parsley
- Dash pepper
- ½ tsp. salt, or to taste
- ½ tsp. cinnamon
- ¼ tsp. allspice
- ¼ tsp. nutmeg
- 1½ tbsp. margarine, melted
- 1-2 tbsp. vegetable oil, for frying

Directions:

Preheat oven to 350°.

In a medium mixing bowl, knead together all the ingredients except the oil until well mixed and smooth. With wet hands, form the mixture into 1-inch balls.

In a frying pan, heat part of the oil. Fry about a third of the balls at a time on medium high, shaking the pan to keep the balls rounded and browning on all sides. Cook until brown all over. Drain on paper toweling and then put in a 2-quart casserole. Brown the remaining turkey balls in batches, using more oil if necessary.

When all the meatballs are browned, bake the casserole for 30 minutes to complete cooking. If you prefer, refrigerate the casserole to pull out and finish cooking just before serving. These are good both hot and cold.

Spaghetti and Meatballs

A classic spaghetti and meatballs recipe.

Makes: 8 servings

Prep: 35 mins

Cook: 45 mins

Ingredients:

- 4 slices bread
- ½ cup milk
- 2 pounds lean ground beef
- 2 large eggs, beaten
- 1 cup (4 ounces) grated Parmesan cheese
- ⅓ cup chopped fresh parsley
- ½ tsp. dried oregano
- ½ tsp. dried basil
- 3 cloves garlic, finely chopped
- Salt and freshly ground black pepper
- Olive oil, for frying the meatballs
- 2 jars (24 to 26 ounces each) gluten-free pasta sauce
- 1 pound spaghetti

Directions:

Toast the bread, then let it cool. Break the bread into fine crumbs with your fingers. Place the crumbs in a small bowl and stir in the milk. Let the breadcrumbs soak up the milk, 8 to 10 minutes.

Meanwhile, place the ground beef, prosciutto, if using, eggs, ½ cup of the Parmesan cheese, and the parsley, oregano, basil, garlic, and 1 tsp. of salt in a large bowl. Season with black pepper to taste. Using clean hands, gently combine the meat mixture to distribute the herbs and incorporate the eggs. Add the soaked breadcrumbs &, using your hands, gently work the soaked crumbs into the meatball mixture. Don't overwork. Divide the meat mixture into approximately ¼ cup– size meatballs; you will have 16 to 20 meatballs. You can make smaller meatballs, if desired.

Line a platter with paper towels. Place 2 to 3 tbsp. of olive oil in a large, deep frying pan over medium heat. When the oil is hot, place half of the meatballs in the pan and brown them on all sides, using a large spoon to turn them as they brown, 7 to 8 minutes. Transfer the browned meatballs to the paper towel–lined platter to drain. Cook the second batch of meatballs the same way, adding more olive oil to the pan first, if needed.

Discard the cooking oil from the pan and wipe out the pan. Pour the gluten-free pasta sauce into the pan and let it come to a simmer over low heat, 4 to 5 minutes. Add the meatballs to the pan, spoon the sauce over them, and let them simmer until they are cooked through, 20 to 25 minutes.

Bring a large pot of water to boil over high heat and add ½ tsp. salt. When the water is boiling add the spaghetti & cook, until the spaghetti is just done 8 to 10 minutes. Drain the spaghetti and rinse it briefly with cold water to stop the cooking process. Drain the spaghetti again and return it to the pot. Toss the spaghetti with 1 tbsp. of olive oil.

Serve the spaghetti on the side of the sauce and meatballs, passing the remaining ½ cup of Parmesan cheese for spooning on top.

Notes: Prosciutto is thinly sliced Italian ham. You can omit it, if desired, although it does lend a more authentic Italian flavor to the meatballs. And as far as choosing the right gluten-free spaghetti, use the best you can find; one made of brown rice, or a mix of rice and corn, is fine.

Maple-Ginger Chicken Meatballs

Sweet and salty meatballs with maple syrup and ginger.

Makes: 4 servings

Prep: 10 mins

Cook: 15 mins

Ingredients:

- ¾ pound (300 g) ground chicken
- ¼ cup (30 g) Japanese panko breadcrumbs
- 2 tbsp. maple syrup
- 1 tsp. grated fresh ginger
- 1 large egg, beaten
- ½ tsp. sesame oil
- ¼ tsp. salt

Directions:

Preheat oven to 425°F. Line a baking pan aluminum foil.

Meanwhile, place all the ingredients in a large bowl. Using your hands, gently mix until everything is well combined.

Shape the mixture into cherry-size balls and arrange them in a single layer on the rimmed baking sheet. Bake for 10 to 15 mins, shaking the baking sheet halfway through cooking, until the meatballs are golden brown with an internal temperature of 165°F/75°C.

Poached Beef Meatballs

These quick-to-make, flavorful meatballs are poached right in the noodle broth. To keep them fluffy rather than dense, use a light hand when mixing and shaping them.

Makes: 4 servings

Prep: 10 mins

Cook: 10 mins

Ingredients:

- ½ pound (230 g) ground beef
- 1 tsp. soy sauce
- 2 tbsp. oyster sauce
- 1 garlic clove, grated
- Broth, for cooking and serving

Directions:

Mix all above ingredients in a bowl; mix thoroughly. Roll this mixture into small balls, roughly the size of a maraschino cherry.

Bring a pot of broth to a rapid simmer. Carefully slip the meatballs into the pot and cook until firm, about 3 minutes.

Chicken Meatballs

These little skewered chicken meatballs are the perfect pre-game starter.

Makes: 20 meatballs

Prep: 15 mins

Cook: 20 mins

Ingredients:

- 1 lb. chicken mince, preferably thigh meat
- 3 spring onions, thinly cut at an angle
- 2 tsp. garlic, peeled and grated
- 1 tbsp. ginger, peeled and grated
- 1 egg, beaten
- 50g (2oz) panko breadcrumbs
- 2 tsp. whole milk
- 2 tbsp. gochujang (Korean chili paste)
- 1 tsp. soy sauce
- 2 tsp. brown sugar
- 11/2 tsp. sea salt
- 1/2 tsp. black pepper
- 3 tbsp. plain flour
- Vegetable oil, for frying

To Serve

- A pinch of roasted black sesame seeds
- Sriracha or Gochujang Mayonnaise, for dipping

Directions:

For meatballs, in a bowl, mix together the chicken mince, spring onions, garlic, ginger, egg, panko, milk, gochujang, soy sauce, brown sugar, salt and pepper. Form the mixture into about 20 golf ball-sized (35g/1 1/4oz) meatballs.

Spoon the flour onto a plate, then roll the meatballs in the flour, shaking off the excess.

Heat a non-stick frying pan on a med–high heat. Drizzle generously with oil. Working in batches so as not to overcrowd the pan, place the meatballs in the pan & fry for about 5–6 mins, until cooked through, rotating often to cook evenly.

Serve the meatballs immediately with skewers, garnished with chives and sesame seeds, with Sriracha or gochujang mayonnaise on the side.

Honey-Ginger Chicken Meatballs

Sweet and salty meatballs with honey and ginger.

Makes: 4 servings

Prep: 10 mins

Cook: 15 mins

Ingredients:

- ¾ pound (300 g) ground chicken
- ¼ cup (30 g) Japanese panko breadcrumbs
- 2 tbsp. honey
- 1 tsp. grated fresh ginger
- 1 large egg, beaten
- ½ tsp. sesame oil
- ¼ tsp. salt

Directions:

Preheat oven to 425°F. Line a baking pan aluminum foil.

Meanwhile, place all the ingredients in a large bowl. Using your hands, gently mix until everything is well combined.

Shape the mixture into cherry-size balls and arrange them in a single layer on the rimmed baking sheet. Bake for 10 to 15 mins, shaking the baking sheet halfway through cooking, until the meatballs are golden brown with an internal temperature of 165°F/75°C.

Persian Meatball Soup

Persian inspired chicken wings meatball soup recipe.

Makes: 6 servings

Prep: 10 mins

Cook: 1 hr. 10 mins

Ingredients:

- 1/4 cup canola oil
- 1 lb. chicken wings
- Salt & freshly ground black pepper, to taste
- 3 medium carrots, roughly chopped
- 3 medium onions (two roughly chopped, one minced)
- 8 cups chicken stock
- 2 garlic cloves, crushed
- 1 bay leaf
- 1 1/2 lbs. ground chicken
- 1 1/2 cups chickpea flour
- 2 1/2 tsp. ground turmeric
- 2 tsp ground coriander
- 1 1/2 tsp. baking soda
- 1/2 tsp. ground cardamom

Directions:

Place a soup pot over medium heat. Heat 3 tbsp. of oil in it.

Sprinkle some salt & pepper over the chicken wings. Brown it in the pot for 14 min. Stir in the onions, carrots, and garlic. Sauté them for 10 min.

Stir in the stock, bay leaf, and salt. Cook them until they start boiling. Lower the heat & cook the soup for 37 min.

Pour the broth in a colander and drain it. Discard the chicken wings with veggies. Pour the broth into the pot.

Heat the oil in a large pan. Add the onion and cook them for 5 min. Allow it to cool down slightly.

Get a large mixing bowl: Combine in it the rest of the ingredients and mix them well. Shape the mix into meatballs.

Stir the meatballs into the hot broth. Cook them until they start simmering. Put on half a cover over the pot. Cook the soup for 18 min. Serve your soup warm.

Potato and Pepper Meatballs

Potato, saffron, bell pepper meatball recipe.

Makes: 6 servings

Prep: 10 mins

Cook: 20 mins

Ingredients:

- 5 potatoes
- 1 medium green bell pepper, chopped
- 4 eggs
- 1/4 tsp. saffron
- 1/2 tsp. baking powder
- Oil

Directions:

Take a salted pot of water to boil. Cook in it the potato until it becomes soft. Drain it and place it aside.

Place the potato in a grater and grate it.

Get a large mixing bowl: Mix in it the potato with eggs, bell pepper, a pinch of salt and pepper. Mix them well. Add the saffron with baking powder. Mix them again.

Place a large skillet over medium heat. Heat the oil in it. Shape the mix into balls and cook them in the pan for 10 min on each side with the lid on.

Serve your potato meatballs warm.

Persian Lentils and Meatballs Soup

Persian-inspired lentils and meatball soup recipe.

Makes: 4-6 servings

Prep: 10 mins

Cook: 1 hr. 20 mins

Ingredients:

Soup

- 1/4 cup lentils
- 1/4 cup dried black-eyed peas
- 4 -5 cup water
- 1 1/2 tsp. salt
- 1 C. fine egg noodles
- 1/2 cup chopped parsley

Meatballs

- Half lb. ground beef
- 1/4 tsp. cinnamon
- 1/4 tsp. fine grind black pepper
- 1/3 cup finely chopped onions
- 1/2 tsp. salt

Spice Garnish

- 2 tsp. dried mint
- 1/2 tsp. black pepper
- 1/4 tsp. cinnamon

Directions:

Place a large pot of water over medium heat with a pinch of salt. Cook in it the beans with lentils for 38 min. Stir in the parsley with noodles.

Get a large mixing bowl: Combine in it the meatballs ingredients and mix them well. Shape the mix into meatballs. Add them to the pot and cook them for 35 min.

Get a mortar: Crush in it the mint with cinnamon and pepper. Sprinkle it over the soup then serve it warm.

Kashk Lamb Meatballs Stew

Authentic Persian Kashk lamb meatball stew recipe.

Makes: 6 servings

Prep: 4 hr. 10 mins

Cook: 1 hr.

Ingredients:

- 1/2 lb. ground lamb
- 50 g dried black-eye beans
- ¼ cup dried brown lentils
- 1 cup of fresh mint
- 4 1/2 cups fresh spinach
- 50 g dried split peas
- 2 onions
- 1 cup kashk
- 1/4 tsp pomegranate powder
- Vegetable oil
- Salt
- Black pepper

Directions:

Rinse the black-eye beans, split-peas, and lentils. Put them in a bowl & top with water. Place them aside to soak for 4 h 10 min.

Rinse them and drain them. Place them in large saucepan with 4 1/4 C. of water with a pinch of salt. Cook them for 22 min over medium heat until 1 C. of liquid is left.

Get a large mixing bowl: Grate the onion and add to it the lamb with a pinch of salt and pepper. Mix them well. Shape the mix into meatballs.

Place a large pan over medium heat. Heat a splash of oil in it. Brown in it the meatballs for 4 min.

Rinse the spinach with some cool water and chop them. Stir them into the saucepan with the beans mix and meatballs. Cook them for 18 min. Stir in the pomegranate powder.

Place a small skillet over medium heat. Heat a splash of oil in it. Add the mint and fry it. Crush it and use it to garnish the stew. Serve it warm.

Kimchi, Prosciutto, and Chive Jeon

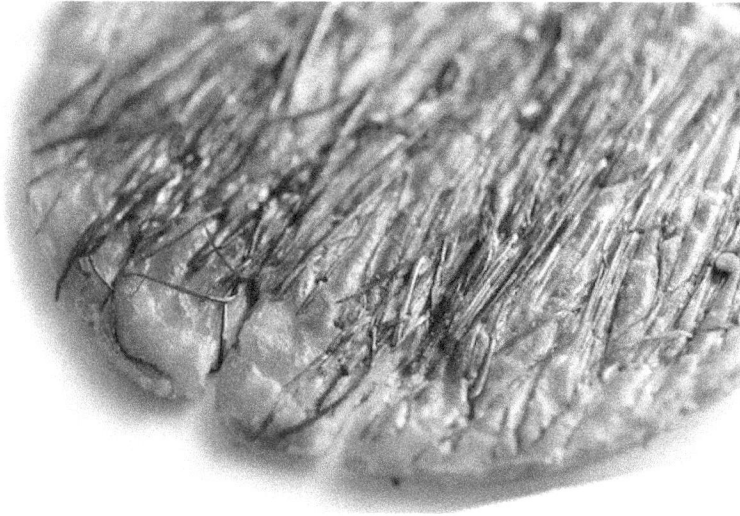

These little flat meatballs are so easy to make, and are often served at room temperature, so they are perfect for lunches or for a quick snack.

Makes: 8 servings

Prep: 10 mins

Cook: 20 mins

Ingredients:

- 6oz beef mince
- 1 3/4oz prosciutto, finely chopped
- 3 1/2oz tofu, drained and pressed to remove excess water (shown here)
- 1 1/4oz cabbage kimchi, finely chopped
- 1/4 tsp garlic, grated/finely chopped
- 1/4 tsp ginger, peeled and grated
- 2 shallots, finely chopped
- 4 tbsp. chives, finely chopped, + extra to serve
- 1 tsp roasted sesame oil
- 1 tsp roasted sesame seeds
- 1 tsp gochugaru (Korean chili flakes)
- 2 tsp mirin
- 2 eggs
- A pinch of salt
- 3 3/4oz rice flour
- Vegetable oil, for frying
- Pancake Dipping Sauce, to serve

Directions:

In a bowl, mix beef, prosciutto, tofu (it will crumble as you mix), kimchi, garlic, ginger, shallots, chives, pepper, sesame oil, sesame seeds, gochugaru and mirin. Season to taste.

Crack the 2 eggs into a bowl, add the pinch of salt and beat well. Set aside. Put the rice flour in another bowl and set aside.

Using your hands, shape the meat mixture into small patties, about 50g (2oz) each. Dredge each patty in the rice flour, shaking off the excess, and place on a tray.

Heat a non-stick frying pan on a med–low heat and drizzle with oil. Dip each into the egg mixture, then place carefully into the pan. Fry for about 4–5 mins until cooked through, flipping once.

Serve immediately with the dipping sauce and sprinkle with fresh chives to garnish.

Sweet Potato Bell Pepper Meatballs

Sweet potato, saffron, bell pepper meatball recipe.

Makes: 6 servings

Prep: 10 mins

Cook: 20 mins

Ingredients:

- 5 sweet potatoes
- 1 medium green bell pepper, chopped
- 4 eggs
- 1/4 tsp saffron
- 1/2 tsp baking powder
- Oil

Directions:

Take a salted pot of water to boil. Cook in it the potato until it becomes soft. Drain it and place it aside.

Place the sweet potato in a grater and grate it.

Get a large mixing bowl: Mix in it the potato with eggs, bell pepper, a pinch of salt and pepper. Mix them well. Add the saffron with baking powder. Mix them again.

Place a large skillet over medium heat. Heat the oil in it. Shape the mix into balls and cook them in the pan for 10 min on each side with the lid on.

Serve your potato meatballs warm.

Beef Meatballs Stew

Beef meatball stew recipe with lentils and spinach.

Makes: 6 servings

Prep: 4 hr. 10 mins

Cook: 1 hr.

Ingredients:

- 1/2 lb. ground beef
- ¼ cup dried black-eye beans
- ¼ cup dried brown lentils
- 1 cup of fresh mint
- 4 1/2 cups fresh spinach
- ¼ cup dried split peas
- 2 onions
- 1 cup kashk
- 1/4 tsp pomegranate powder
- Vegetable oil
- Salt
- Black pepper

Directions:

Rinse the black-eye beans, split-peas, and lentils. Put them in a bowl & top with water. Place them aside to soak for 4 h 10 min.

Rinse them and drain them. Place them in large saucepan with 4 1/4 C. of water with a pinch of salt. Cook them for 22 min over medium heat until 1 C. of liquid is left.

Get a large mixing bowl: Grate the onion and add to it the beef with a pinch of salt and pepper. Mix them well. Shape the mix into meatballs.

Place a large pan over medium heat. Heat a splash of oil in it. Brown in it the meatballs for 4 min.

Rinse the spinach with some cool water and chop them. Stir them into the saucepan with the beans mix and meatballs. Cook them for 18 min. Stir in the pomegranate powder.

Place a small skillet over medium heat. Heat oil in it. Add the mint and fry it. Crush it and use it to garnish the stew. Serve it warm.

Shaami Kebab

Crispy meat shells filled with a surprise center come together to form these Pakistani classic meatballs.

Makes: 20 Kebabs

Prep: 20 mins

Cook: 15 mins

Ingredients:

Meat:

- 2 lb. beef
- 5 cups water
- 1 cup gram lentils, washed through
- ½ cumin powder
- 10 dried red chili pods
- ½ tsp cardamom powder
- 1 tsp black pepper
- 12 garlic cloves, crushed
- ½ tsp cinnamon
- 1 small piece ginger, finely chopped
- ½ tsp cilantro seeds
- 1 tbsp. yogurt
- 1 egg, beaten
- Salt to taste

Filling:

- ½ cup fresh cilantro
- 1 inch piece ginger
- ½ cup fresh mint
- 1 large onion

Directions:

In a large saucepan, combine all the meat ingredients except for the egg. Bring the mixture to a boil. Continue cooking once meat turns tender and is completely cooked through. Remove from heat and allow to cool.

As the meat cooks, prepare the filling. Place all ingredients into a chopper and process till finely chopped. Remove and set aside.

Add in the meat mixture and process until smooth.

Remove into a bowl and add in the beaten egg. Mix well until thoroughly combined.

To start making the kebabs, take about 2 tbsp. of the meat mixture and roll it into a ball. Flatten it lightly and using your finger, create a small indent in the center. Add about a tsp of the filling mixture and cover with the sides, creating a round shape. Flatten to create a thick disk.

Repeat with the rest of the mixture.

To fry the kebabs, heat about 2 tbsp. oil in a frying pan and place kebabs in. Fry on both sides about 2-3 minutes until crispy and golden.

Garnish with cilantro leaves and onion slices and serve.

Chicken Teriyaki Meatballs

Delicious and moist meatballs that are super simple to make!

Makes: 6 servings

Prep: 10 mins

Cook: 25 mins

Ingredients:

- 1 lb. minced chicken
- 4 tbsp. teriyaki sauce
- 1/2 tsp grated gingerroot (optional)
- 2 green onions, sliced
- Garlic salt

Directions:

Preheat oven to 350 F.

Get a large mixing bowl: Combine in it all the ingredients. Mix them well. Shape the mix into 1 inch meatballs.

Place meatballs on a lined baking sheet. Cook them in the oven for 28 min. Serve them warm.

Mongolian Beef Meatballs

These meatballs are the beef version of the previously mentioned chicken meatballs but just as delicious!

Makes: 6 servings

Prep: 10 mins

Cook: 25 mins

Ingredients:

- 1 lb. minced beef
- 4 tbsp. teriyaki sauce
- 1/2 tsp grated gingerroot (optional)
- 2 green onions, sliced
- Garlic salt

Directions:

Preheat oven to 350 F.

Get a large mixing bowl: Combine in it all the ingredients. Mix them well. Shape the mix into 1 inch meatballs.

Place meatballs on a lined baking sheet. Cook them in the oven for 28 min. Serve them warm.

Portuguese Sausage Meatballs

Packed with spice and garlic, Portuguese sausage meatballs is the perfect addition to your plate!

Makes: 6 servings

Prep: 10 mins plus overnight

Cook: 20 mins

Ingredients:

- 1 pound well-marbled ground beef
- 4 garlic cloves, peeled and finely grated
- 1 or 2 Hawaiian chili peppers, finely minced
- ½ tsp. Portuguese Spice Blend
- 1 tbsp. paprika
- ½ tbsp. kosher salt
- 1 tsp. freshly ground black pepper
- 2 tbsp. red wine vinegar
- Neutral oil, for frying

Directions:

In large bowl, combine the beef, garlic, chili pepper, spice blend, paprika, salt, pepper, and vinegar and mix with a wooden spoon or heavy spatula until well combined. Cover the bowl with plastic wrap and refrigerate for 24 hours to allow the flavors to meld and mellow.

The next day, scoop up about 2 tbsp. of meat and shape it into a ball. Flatten the ball with the palms of your hands to form a small, ¼-inch-thick patty. Repeat this process until all the meat has been formed. Be sure to place a piece of parchment between the patties if you are layering them. (The patties can be stored in the refrigerator in a covered container for 3 to 4 days or frozen for up to 1 month.)

Warm a tbsp. or two of oil in a skillet over medium heat and place as many patties as can fit without touching in the pan. Cook for 3 to 4 minutes on each side, until evenly browned and cooked through. Serve immediately.

Finnish Meatballs

Delicious Finnish meatballs recipe.

Makes: 6 servings

Prep: 10 mins

Cook: 10 mins

Ingredients:

- 4 whole wheat bread slices, crumbled
- ½ cup whole milk
- 24 ounces ground beef meat
- 1 egg, whisked
- ½ cup yellow onion, chopped
- ¼ tsp. ground allspice
- Salt and black pepper to the taste
- ¼ tsp. nutmeg powder
- 2 tbsp. butter
- 1 tbsp. white flour
- 2 tbsp. olive oil
- 1 cup chicken stock
- 1 cup fresh cranberries
- ¼ cup heavy cream
- 1 tsp. lemon zest, grated
- 1 tbsp. lemon juice
- 2 tbsp. sugar
- 1 tsp. ginger, grated
- 2 tbsp. dill, chopped
- 2 tbsp. parsley, chopped

Directions:

Put bread in a bowl, add whole milk, soak for 5 minutes, drain well and put in another bowl.

Add beef, egg, onion, nutmeg, allspice, salt and pepper, stir well and shape medium meatballs out of this mixture.

Heat up a pan with half of the oil and half of the butter over medium heat, add the meatballs, cook them for 4 minutes on each side and transfer them to a plate.

Heat up another pan with the rest of the oil and the rest of the butter over medium heat, add the flour and whisk it well.

Add stock, salt, pepper and cream, stir, bring to a simmer over medium low heat, add the meatballs and cook them for 10 minutes.

In your food processor, mix cranberries with lemon zest, lemon juice, sugar, ginger, salt, pepper, dill and parsley and pulse well.

Divide the meatballs mix between plates, add the cranberry sauce on the side and serve.

Ginger Beef Meatballs

Sweet and salty meatballs with maple syrup and ginger.

Makes: 4 servings

Prep: 10 mins

Cook: 15 mins

Ingredients:

- ¾ pound (300 g) ground beef
- ¼ cup (30 g) Japanese panko breadcrumbs
- 2 tbsp. maple syrup
- 1 tsp. grated fresh ginger
- 1 large egg, beaten
- ½ tsp. sesame oil
- ¼ tsp. salt

Directions:

Preheat oven to 425°F. Line a baking pan aluminum foil.

Meanwhile, place all the ingredients in a large bowl. Using your hands, gently mix until everything is well combined.

Shape the mixture into cherry-size balls and arrange them in a single layer on the rimmed baking sheet. Bake for 10 to 15 mins, shaking the baking sheet halfway through cooking, until the meatballs are golden brown with an internal temperature of 165°F/75°C.

Chicken Meatballs Stew

Chicken meatball stew recipe with lentils, Kashk and spinach.

Makes: 6 servings

Prep: 4 hr. 10 mins

Cook: 1 hr.

Ingredients:

- 1/2 lb. ground chicken
- ¼ cup dried black-eye beans
- ¼ cup dried brown lentils
- 1 cup of fresh mint
- 4 1/2 cups fresh spinach
- ¼ cup dried split peas
- 2 onions
- 1 cup kashk
- 1/4 tsp pomegranate powder
- Vegetable oil
- Salt
- Black pepper

Directions:

Rinse the black-eye beans, split-peas, and lentils. Put them in a bowl & top with water. Place them aside to soak for 4 h 10 min.

Rinse them and drain them. Place them in large saucepan with 4 1/4 C. of water with a pinch of salt. Cook them for 22 min over medium heat until 1 C. of liquid is left.

Get a large mixing bowl: Grate the onion and add to it the chicken with a pinch of salt and pepper. Mix them well. Shape the mix into meatballs.

Place a large pan over medium heat. Heat a splash of oil in it. Brown in it the meatballs for 4 min.

Rinse the spinach with some cool water and chop them. Stir them into the saucepan with the beans mix and meatballs. Cook them for 18 min. Stir in the pomegranate powder.

Place a small skillet over medium heat. Heat oil in it. Add the mint and fry it. Crush it and use it to garnish the stew. Serve it warm.

Honey Beef Meatballs

Sweet and salty meatballs with honey and ginger.

Makes: 4 servings

Prep: 10 mins

Cook: 15 mins

Ingredients:

- ¾ pound ground beef
- ¼ cup Japanese panko breadcrumbs
- 2 tbsp. honey
- 1 tsp. grated fresh ginger
- 1 large egg, beaten
- ½ tsp. sesame oil
- ¼ tsp. salt

Directions:

Preheat oven to 425°F. Line a baking pan aluminum foil.

Meanwhile, place all the ingredients in a large bowl. Using your hands, gently mix until everything is well combined.

Shape the mixture into cherry-size balls and arrange them in a single layer on the rimmed baking sheet. Bake for 10 to 15 mins, shaking the baking sheet halfway through cooking, until the meatballs are golden brown.

Mediterranean Beef Meatballs

Meatballs with Mediterranean-inspired flavors.

Makes: 4 servings

Prep: 10 mins

Cook: 45 mins

Ingredients:

- 1¼ pounds ground beef
- ½ cup grated onion
- 1 egg, beaten
- 1½ tbsp. chopped raisins
- 1 tbsp. chopped walnuts or pecans
- 1 tbsp. minced fresh parsley
- Dash pepper
- ½ tsp. salt, or to taste
- ½ tsp. cinnamon
- ¼ tsp. allspice
- ¼ tsp. nutmeg
- 1½ tbsp. margarine, melted
- 1 to 2 tbsp. vegetable oil, for frying

Directions:

Preheat oven to 350°.

In a medium mixing bowl, knead together all the ingredients except the oil until well mixed and smooth. With wet hands, form the mixture into 1-inch balls.

In a frying pan, heat part of the oil. Fry about a third of the balls at a time on medium high, shaking the pan to keep the balls rounded and browning on all sides. Cook until brown all over. Drain on paper toweling and then put in a 2-quart casserole. Brown the remaining meatballs in batches, using more oil if necessary.

When all the meatballs are browned, bake the casserole for 30 minutes to complete cooking. If you prefer, refrigerate the casserole to pull out and finish cooking just before serving. These are good both hot and cold.

Conclusion

Well, there you have it! 30 delicious meatball recipes for you to try! Try out each and every recipe to get the full benefit from this book and make sure to share with your friends and family

About the Author

Allie Allen developed her passion for the culinary arts at the tender age of five when she would help her mother cook for their large family of 8. Even back then, her family knew this would be more than a hobby for the young Allie and when she graduated from high school, she applied to cooking school in London. It had always been a dream of the young chef to study with some of Europe's best and she made it happen by attending the Chef Academy of London.

After graduation, Allie decided to bring her skills back to North America and open up her own restaurant. After 10 successful years as head chef and owner, she decided to sell her business and pursue other career avenues. This monumental decision led Allie to her true calling, teaching. She also started to write e-books for her students to study at home for practice. She is now the proud author of several e-books and gives private and semi-private cooking lessons to a range of students at all levels of experience.

Stay tuned for more from this dynamic chef and teacher when she releases more informative e-books on cooking and baking in the near future. Her work is infused with stores and anecdotes you will love!

Author's Afterthoughts

I can't tell you how grateful I am that you decided to read my book. My most heartfelt thanks that you took time out of your life to choose my work and I hope you find benefit within these pages.

There are so many books available today that offer similar content so that makes it even more humbling that you decided to buying mine.

Tell me what you thought! I am eager to hear your opinion and ideas on what you read as are others who are looking for a good book to buy. Leave a review on Amazon.com so others can benefit from your wisdom!

With much thanks,

Allie Allen

CPSIA information can be obtained
at www.ICGtesting.com
Printed in the USA
LVHW110208190220
647432LV00023B/88

9 781674 595962